STEVE JAY

Crown of Midnight Stars

Contents

The Mysterious Prophecy

The night was shrouded in an ink-black darkness, broken only by the faint glow of stars scattered across the vast canvas of the sky. In a secluded cottage nestled deep within the ancient woods, a young mage named Elara sat hunched over an ancient tome, her eyes scanning the cryptic symbols that adorned its pages. The air crackled with an electric charge, and a feeling of anticipation hung heavy in the room. The flames in the fireplace danced wildly, casting eerie shadows on the walls.

Elara's hands trembled as she traced her fingers over the faded runes, her mind racing to decipher the meaning behind the mysterious words. The wind outside howled like a mournful spirit, rattling the windows as if urging her to unravel the secrets hidden within the pages.

With bated breath, Elara whispered the incantation, her voice barely audible above the wind's lament. The room seemed to pulse with magic, and suddenly, the words on the pages came to life, glowing with an ethereal light. The ancient prophecy revealed itself to her, its meaning slowly unfolding like the petals of a forbidden flower.

"In the heart of shadows, where moonlight weaves,
  A crown of midnight stars, the bravest heart conceives.
  Through trials of fire and trials of ice,
  One shall seek it, one shall pay the price."

Elara's heart quickened with excitement and trepidation. The words spoke of a crown, a powerful artifact said to grant unimaginable abilities to its bearer. But obtaining it would not come without a cost, a price that was yet to be revealed. The prophecy was a riddle, a tantalizing enigma that demanded to be solved.

The young mage's thoughts were interrupted by a sudden knock on the door, sharp and urgent. Elara's pulse quickened, her hand instinctively reaching for the staff leaning against the table. With cautious steps, she approached the door, her senses heightened, attuned to the subtlest of disturbances.

"Who's there?" Elara called out, her voice steady despite the adrenaline surging through her veins.

"It's me, Seraphine," a hushed voice replied from the other side of the door.

Relief washed over Elara as she recognized the voice of her trusted friend and fellow mage. She quickly unbarred the door, allowing Seraphine to enter. The woman's cloak billowed with the force of the wind as she stepped inside, her eyes wide with urgency.

"Elara, you've found it, haven't you?" Seraphine's voice was a breathless whisper, her gaze fixed on the glowing pages of the ancient tome.

Elara nodded, her excitement tempered by the weight of the prophecy's words. "The Crown of Midnight Stars," she said, her voice barely more than a murmur. "But there's more to it, Seraphine. Something we're missing."

Seraphine's eyes narrowed, her brows furrowing in concentration. "We need to find out what the trials of fire and ice signify," she said, her mind already racing with possibilities.

As if in response to their conversation, the room suddenly grew cold, the temperature dropping dramatically. Frost formed on the windows, creeping across the glass like skeletal fingers. Elara and Seraphine exchanged a knowing glance, their senses on high alert.

"We're not alone," Seraphine said, her voice a mere breath in the icy air.

A shadow moved in the corner of the room, a silhouette darker than the night itself. Elara's grip tightened on her staff as a figure emerged from the darkness, their face obscured by a hooded cloak.

"I've been searching for the Crown of Midnight Stars for years," the stranger said, their voice low and chilling. "And I won't let you stand in my way."

Elara's heart pounded in her chest as she faced the mysterious intruder. The room seemed to close in around them, the very walls whispering secrets of ancient power and long-forgotten magic. The battle for the crown had begun, and in the depths of the night, amidst shadows and secrets, the fate of the world hung in the balance.

And so, the three mages stood in a silent standoff, each aware of the stakes, each harboring their own secrets and desires. The air crackled with tension, and the suspense was thick enough to touch, as they prepared to embark on a perilous journey that would test their courage, cunning, and loyalty to the very core.

The Enigmatic Guide

The encounter with the mysterious intruder had left Elara, Seraphine, and the stranger in a tense standoff. The room crackled with magical energy, as if the very air were charged with the potential for violence. Elara tightened her grip on her staff, her eyes locked onto the hooded figure.

"You won't find the crown without my help," the stranger said, their voice low and gravelly. "I've studied the ancient texts for years. I know the trials, the tests we must face."

Elara exchanged a wary glance with Seraphine. Despite her distrust, Elara couldn't deny the logic in the stranger's words. The trials mentioned in the prophecy were vague, and deciphering them would be crucial to finding the Crown of Midnight Stars.

"Fine," Elara said, her voice steady. "But we work together. No tricks, no betrayals."

The stranger nodded, pulling back their hood to reveal a weathered face, marked by time and wisdom. "Agreed," they said, their eyes gleaming with an odd mix of determination and sadness.

With a tentative truce established, the three mages set out on their journey, guided by the stranger's knowledge. They traveled through dense forests and across moonlit fields, their path illuminated by the soft glow of the stars above. Along the way, the stranger, who introduced themselves as Kael, shared stories of ancient civilizations and lost magic, weaving a tapestry of intrigue and wonder.

As they ventured deeper into the heart of the enchanted woods, the atmosphere grew thick with mystic energies. Whispers of long-forgotten spells seemed to dance on the wind, and the very trees seemed to watch their progress with ancient, knowing eyes. The world around them came alive with an otherworldly beauty, yet there was an underlying sense of danger that sent shivers down their spines.

"We're nearing the Forbidden Forest," Kael said, his voice low. "Legend has it that it guards the entrance to the first trial."

The Forbidden Forest was a place of dark secrets and elusive mysteries, a realm where reality and illusion intertwined. As they entered its depths, the air grew heavy with enchantment, and the very ground beneath their feet seemed to shift and writhe.

"Stay close," Seraphine warned, her eyes scanning the surroundings for any signs of danger.

But danger came in a form they didn't expect. The forest, sensing their presence, unleashed a series of illusions designed to test their resolve. Shadows danced in the corners of their vision, and the sound of ghostly whispers filled the air. Doubt and fear clawed at their minds, threatening to tear apart the fragile bonds of their alliance.

Elara felt a sudden chill as an apparition appeared before her, taking the form of her long-lost mentor. "You are not worthy," the specter hissed, its voice echoing in her ears. "You will fail, and the crown will be lost forever."

Elara clenched her teeth, banishing the doubts that threatened to consume her. "This is an illusion," she reminded herself, her voice firm. "I won't be swayed by false words."

Seraphine, too, faced her own inner demons. Images of her past mistakes haunted her, taunting her with the possibility of failure. But she stood her ground, her will unyielding. "I've overcome my past," she declared, her voice cutting through the illusion. "I won't let it define me."

Kael, too, faced his fears. The specter of a lost love appeared before him, a painful reminder of a life left behind. But he, too, found the strength to resist the illusion's pull, his eyes burning with determination.

Together, they pressed on, their bond forged through shared challenges and unwavering determination. The illusions grew more potent, more convincing, but they refused to succumb to the forest's tricks. With each step, their confidence grew, and the illusions began to fade, revealing the path forward.

At last, they emerged from the depths of the Forbidden Forest, their clothes tattered and their faces marked by the trials they had faced. But there was a newfound sense of purpose in their eyes, a determination that nothing could break.

"We passed the first trial," Elara said, her voice filled with a mix of relief and pride. "And we'll face whatever comes next together."

With renewed resolve, they continued their journey, guided by the knowledge that they were one step closer to the Crown of Midnight Stars. The world around them pulsed with magic, and the very stars seemed to shine brighter, as if celebrating their victory.

But unknown to them, shadows moved in the periphery of their vision, and unseen forces watched their progress with keen interest. The trials were far from over, and greater challenges lay ahead. As they ventured deeper into the unknown, the suspense grew, the stakes higher than ever before.

And so, under the canopy of a starlit sky, the three mages pressed on, their fates intertwined in a tapestry of magic and destiny. Little did they know that their journey was far from over, and the true test of their courage and resilience was yet to come.

The Forbidden Forest

The moon hung low in the sky, casting a silvery glow over the ancient trees of the Forbidden Forest. Elara, Seraphine, and Kael moved cautiously through the dense foliage, their senses alert to every rustle and whisper. The air was thick with magic, a palpable force that seemed to seep from the very earth beneath their feet.

The forest was alive with strange sounds—ghostly moans, echoing footsteps, and the distant howls of creatures unseen. Each step they took seemed to echo in the eerie silence, raising the hair on the back of their necks. Yet, they pressed on, driven by the urgency of their quest and the knowledge that the next trial awaited them in the heart of this enigmatic realm.

As they ventured deeper, the trees grew taller and more twisted, their branches intertwining like skeletal fingers reaching for the heavens. The very ground beneath them seemed to shift and writhe, as if the forest itself were alive and watching their every move.

"We're close," Kael whispered, his voice barely audible above the wind that rustled the leaves. "The next trial lies ahead. But be warned, the forest is known to play tricks on the mind. Stay focused, and trust no illusion."

His words hung heavy in the air as they continued their journey. The path before them narrowed, the towering trees creating a canopy so dense that only slivers of moonlight penetrated the darkness. Shadows danced around them, their forms flickering like elusive phantoms.

Suddenly, the forest came alive with a cacophony of voices—whispers that seemed to come from all directions, speaking in a language long forgotten. Elara felt a chill creep up her spine as the voices grew louder, their words incomprehensible yet laden with an otherworldly power.

"Ignore them," Seraphine said, her voice steady despite the unease etched on her face. "They're just illusions, meant to distract and confuse."

But Elara couldn't shake the feeling that the voices held a deeper meaning, a message buried within their cryptic words. She strained her ears, trying to decipher the ancient language, her mind racing with possibilities. As she concentrated, the voices seemed to coalesce into a single phrase, repeated like a haunting refrain.

"The heart reveals the truth."

Elara's eyes widened with realization. "The heart," she said, her voice barely more than a whisper. "It's the key to overcoming the illusions. We must trust our instincts, our emotions. They will guide us."

With newfound determination, they pressed on, their senses sharp and their hearts resolute. The forest seemed to sense their purpose, growing darker and more foreboding as they approached the heart of the trial.

At last, they reached a clearing bathed in an eerie, ethereal light. In the center stood a colossal tree, its gnarled roots digging deep into the earth, and its branches reaching toward the sky like the fingers of a giant. At the base of the tree lay a pool of inky black water, its surface so still that it reflected the starlit sky like a mirror.

"This is it," Kael said, his voice hushed with reverence. "The Pool of Reflection. To pass the trial, we must face our deepest fears and doubts. Only then will the path forward be revealed."

Elara felt a knot tighten in her stomach. Facing her fears was no small feat, for her past was marked by loss and regret. Memories of a tragedy long buried rose to the surface, haunting her like vengeful spirits.

Seraphine placed a reassuring hand on Elara's shoulder. "We'll face this together," she said, her eyes filled with unwavering determination.

With a deep breath, Elara stepped toward the pool, her reflection wavering on its dark surface. She closed her eyes, allowing the memories to wash over her like a tidal wave. Faces of loved ones, moments of failure, and the pain of unfulfilled promises—all flooded her mind, threatening to drown her in despair.

But amidst the darkness, a glimmer of hope emerged. The memory of a smile, a whispered promise, and the strength to carry on. Elara clung to these fragments of light, using them to anchor herself in the storm of emotions.

As she opened her eyes, the pool rippled with an unseen force. The reflection of the colossal tree distorted, revealing a hidden passage beneath its roots. Elara turned to Seraphine and Kael, her heart pounding with a mix of fear and triumph.

"We did it," she said, her voice steady despite the turmoil within. "The path forward is beneath the tree. Let's go."

With newfound resolve, they descended into the shadowy passage, their footsteps echoing in the confined space. The air grew colder, and a sense of foreboding settled over them like a suffocating shroud.

The passage led them into a vast chamber adorned with ancient carvings and symbols. At the center stood a pedestal, upon which rested a glowing orb—the embodiment of the forest's magic. It pulsed with an otherworldly light, casting eerie shadows on the chamber walls.

"We've found it," Kael said, his voice filled with awe. "The Heart of the Forest. The source of its power."

But their moment of triumph was short-lived. As Elara reached for the orb, a rumble echoed through the chamber, and the carvings on the walls came to life, depicting scenes of a great cataclysm—a force of unimaginable darkness threatening to consume the world.

"The forest is warning us," Seraphine said, her eyes wide with realization. "The Crown of Midnight Stars is not just a source of power. It's a weapon—one that must be wielded with care, or it could bring about our doom."

Elara felt a chill crawl down her spine. The revelation weighed heavily on her heart, the burden of responsibility settling over her like a leaden mantle. The quest for the crown was not just a matter of personal ambition—it was a matter of world-altering consequence.

With a sense of grim determination, they left the chamber, the Heart of the Forest's warning etched into their minds. The forest seemed to sigh in response, its magic pulsing with a newfound intensity as if acknowledging their understanding.

As they emerged from the Forbidden Forest, the first light of dawn painted the sky in hues of pink and gold. Elara, Seraphine, and Kael stood in the clearing, their faces marked by the trials they had endured. The weight of their knowledge hung heavy in the air, a silent reminder of the challenges that lay ahead.

"We cannot let the power of the Crown fall into the wrong hands," Elara said, her voice resolute. "We must protect it, no matter the cost."

Seraphine nodded, her eyes reflecting the same determination. "Agreed. We'll face whatever comes our way, together."

Kael's gaze was steady, his voice filled with conviction. "The fate of the world rests in our hands. We will not fail."

And so, beneath the dawning sky, the three mages reaffirmed their oath, their destinies intertwined in a tapestry of magic and sacrifice. The suspense of their journey had deepened, the stakes higher than ever before. But they were undeterred, their resolve unyielding as they prepared to face the challenges that lay ahead.

The world was on

the brink of change, and the Crown of Midnight Stars held the key to its fate. Little did they know that their actions would echo through the ages, shaping the course of history in ways they could scarcely imagine. And so, with the weight of the world on their shoulders, they set forth once more, their hearts alight with the fire of purpose and the knowledge that their journey was far from over.

The Rival Mage

The night was alive with a symphony of stars, each twinkle echoing the mysteries that unfolded beneath the cosmic canvas. Elara, Seraphine, and Kael continued their journey, their footsteps muffled by the thick carpet of leaves that covered the forest floor. The air crackled with an electric tension, and an unspoken understanding hung between them—danger lurked at every turn, and they were not the only ones seeking the Crown of Midnight Stars.

Their path led them to the edge of a cliff, overlooking a chasm shrouded in mist. Below, the sound of rushing water echoed like a distant thunderstorm, a reminder of the formidable river that carved its way through the heart of the land.

"We must cross the River of Shadows to reach the next trial," Kael said, his eyes fixed on the swirling waters below. "But be warned, the bridge is guarded by a powerful enchantment. Only those deemed worthy can pass."

Elara's gaze narrowed. "How do we prove our worth?" she asked, her voice steady despite the uncertainty that gnawed at her.

Kael's lips curved into a sly smile. "Through a test of wit and courage," he said. "The Guardian of the Bridge will present us with riddles and challenges. We must solve them to prove our worthiness."

Seraphine raised an eyebrow. "And if we fail?"

Kael's smile faded, replaced by a steely resolve. "We won't," he said, his voice firm. "Failure is not an option."

With a shared nod, they descended the cliffside, their eyes scanning the misty expanse for any signs of movement. The Guardian of the Bridge was said to be a mythical creature, its true form a mystery wrapped in shadows and whispers. As they approached the bridge, a figure emerged from the mist, its silhouette shifting and changing like a mirage.

The Guardian was a creature of ethereal beauty, its form flickering between that of a majestic eagle and a sinuous serpent. Its eyes, however, gleamed with intelligence, a testament to its ancient wisdom.

"You seek passage across my bridge," the Guardian said, its voice a melodic blend of wind and water. "But first, you must prove your worth. Answer my riddles, and the way shall be revealed."

The first riddle came like a gust of wind, swirling around them with enigmatic grace.

"Alive without breath, as cold as death,
    Never thirsty, ever drinking,
    Clad in mail, never clinking.
    What am I?"

Elara furrowed her brow, her mind racing to decipher the puzzle. Seraphine's eyes glinted with understanding, her lips forming a knowing smile. "It's a fish," she said, her voice confident.

The Guardian's eyes glowed with approval. "Correct," it said, its voice echoing through the mist. "You have passed the first test. But there is more to come."

The second riddle flowed from the Guardian's lips, its words weaving a tapestry of mystery.

"The more you take, the more you leave behind.
  What am I?"

Elara's eyes widened with realization. "Footsteps," she said, her voice sure. "The more you walk, the more footsteps you leave behind."

Again, the Guardian nodded, its approval evident. "You have proven your wit," it said. "But the final test awaits."

The third riddle hung in the air, laden with anticipation.

"I speak without a mouth and hear without ears. I have no body, but I come alive with the wind.
  What am I?"

Kael's eyes sparkled with understanding. "An echo," he said, his voice resonating with confidence. "It speaks without a mouth and hears without ears, and it comes alive when sound travels through the wind."

The Guardian's form rippled like a pond disturbed by a stone, its approval washing over them like a gentle breeze. "You have shown great wisdom," it said, its voice softening. "You may pass."

With the Guardian's blessing, they crossed the bridge, their hearts lighter with the knowledge that they had overcome the trial. But their victory was short-lived, for as they stepped onto the other side, a figure emerged from the shadows—a rival mage, his eyes ablaze with a hunger for power.

"Alistair," Elara said, her voice a mixture of surprise and disdain. "What are you doing here?"

Alistair's lips curled into a sneer. "The same thing you are," he said, his voice dripping with malice. "Seeking the Crown of Midnight Stars. But unlike you, I won't let sentimentality cloud my judgment. I will use its power to reshape the world in my image."

Seraphine's eyes narrowed, her staff at the ready. "You underestimate the danger," she warned. "The crown is not a mere tool. It's a force that could bring about destruction if wielded without caution."

Alistair scoffed, his arrogance undiminished. "I don't need a lecture from you," he said, his voice laced with contempt. "I know what I'm doing. And I won't let anyone stand in my way."

With a flick of his wrist, Alistair conjured a wall of fire, its flames dancing with a deadly elegance. Elara, Seraphine, and Kael scrambled to defend themselves, their magical shields forming a protective barrier against the searing heat.

The battle that ensued was fierce and unrelenting, a clash of power and wills that shook the very foundation of the bridge. Spells and counterspells filled the air, their brilliance illuminating the mist-shrouded night. Each mage fought with a determination born of conviction, their hearts ablaze with the knowledge that the outcome would shape the course of their destinies.

Elara's magic crackled like lightning, her spells striking with precision and force. Seraphine's control over the elements was a sight to behold, the wind and water bending to her command. Kael, too, proved his mettle, his knowledge of ancient spells a formidable weapon in their arsenal.

But Alistair was no ordinary foe. His spells were cunning and unpredictable, his mastery over the dark arts evident in every incantation. The battle raged on, neither side willing to yield, each moment escalating the suspense to unbearable heights.

In a final, desperate gambit, Alistair unleashed a torrent of shadowy energy, its power threatening to consume everything in its path. Elara, Seraphine, and Kael combined their strength, their magic colliding with the darkness in a cataclysmic explosion.

The force of their combined attack sent shockwaves through the bridge, shattering the enchantments that held it together. The ground trembled beneath their feet, and the chasm below yawned wide, threatening to swallow them whole.

With a cry of desperation, Elara reached out, her magic forming a protective bubble around them. The bridge collapsed into the abyss, its remnants disappearing into the darkness below. The world seemed to hold its breath, the suspense of the moment stretching into eternity.

When the dust settled and the echoes of battle faded, Elara, Seraphine, and Kael found themselves standing on the edge of the chasm, their hearts pounding with adrenaline. Alistair was nowhere to be seen, his fate a mystery lost in the

depths of the abyss.

"We did it," Seraphine said, her voice filled with a mixture of relief and exhaustion. "But at what cost?"

Elara's gaze was steely, her resolve unyielding. "We cannot afford to falter," she said, her voice firm. "We must continue our quest. The Crown of Midnight Stars is our only hope."

And so, with the memory of their battle against Alistair etched into their minds, they pressed on, their determination unshaken by the challenges they had faced. The suspense of their journey had deepened, the stakes higher than ever before. But they were undeterred, their resolve unbreakable as they prepared to face the trials that lay ahead.

The world was on the brink of change, and the Crown of Midnight Stars held the key to its fate. Little did they know that their actions would echo through the ages, shaping the course of history in ways they could scarcely imagine. And so, with the weight of the world on their shoulders, they set forth once more, their hearts alight with the fire of purpose and the knowledge that their journey was far from over.

The Lost Temple

The night was alive with a tapestry of stars, each one a distant promise of the mysteries that lay ahead. Elara, Seraphine, and Kael journeyed deeper into the heart of the ancient forest, their footsteps muffled by the thick undergrowth. The air was thick with enchantment, and a sense of foreboding hung heavy in the night.

Their path led them to the foot of a colossal mountain, its peak shrouded in clouds that whispered secrets of forgotten ages. At the mountain's base lay the entrance to the Lost Temple—an ancient, mythical place rumored to hold the key to the final trial in their quest for the Crown of Midnight Stars.

The entrance to the temple was marked by a massive stone door, adorned with intricate carvings depicting gods and mythical creatures. Its surface was smooth, as if worn down by centuries of wind and rain. Elara traced her fingers over the carvings, her senses tingling with the touch of ancient magic.

"This is it," Kael said, his voice a hushed whisper. "The entrance to the Lost Temple. But beware, for the temple is said to be guarded by powerful traps and illusions. We must tread carefully."

With a shared nod, they pushed open the stone door, its weight surprisingly light against their combined strength. The air inside the temple was cool and musty, laden with the scent of ancient stone and forgotten incense. Torches flickered along the walls, casting eerie shadows that danced to the rhythm of their footsteps.

As they ventured deeper into the temple, the walls came alive with carvings that seemed to move and shift, telling stories of gods and heroes, of trials and tribulations. The very stones beneath their feet seemed to pulse with a heartbeat, as if the temple itself were a living, breathing entity.

"We must be cautious," Seraphine warned, her eyes scanning the surroundings for any signs of danger. "Illusions could be hiding in plain sight, waiting to deceive us."

Elara nodded, her senses on high alert. The suspense was thick in the air, a tangible presence that raised the hairs on the back of their necks. Each step they took seemed to echo in the vast chamber, their movements deliberate and measured.

Suddenly, the temple came alive with a blinding flash of light, and the ground trembled beneath their feet. The walls seemed to warp and twist, and the very floor seemed to vanish, leaving them suspended in a void of darkness.

"This is an illusion," Kael said, his voice calm despite the uncertainty of their situation. "We must focus on what is real. Our conviction will break the illusion's hold."

With steely determination, they closed their eyes and concentrated on their inner strength, blocking out the illusion's deceptive imagery. Slowly, the darkness began to fade, revealing the true form of the chamber—a grand hall adorned with pillars of marble and tapestries that told the story of the temple's creation.

But their respite was short-lived. The ground beneath them rumbled once more, and a horde of spectral warriors materialized out of thin air, their eyes ablaze with a hunger for battle.

"We are not alone," Elara said, her voice low. "These warriors are a testament to the temple's defenses. We must defeat them to proceed."

The battle that followed was like a whirlwind of steel and magic, their skills and determination pitted against the illusionary warriors. Elara's staff crackled with energy, her spells striking with precision and force. Seraphine summoned gusts of wind and torrents of water, her control over the elements unmatched. Kael's knowledge of ancient spells proved invaluable, his incantations unraveling the illusions that bound the spectral warriors.

With every defeated foe, the chamber seemed to tremble with approval, as if acknowledging their prowess. Yet, the suspense hung heavy in the air, for they knew that the temple's true challenges were yet to come.

As they pressed deeper into the temple, the architecture grew more elaborate, the carvings more intricate. They found themselves in a grand chamber, its ceiling adorned with a mural depicting a celestial battle between gods and demons. At the center of the chamber stood a pedestal, upon which rested a glowing gem—the final trial in their quest for the Crown of Midnight Stars.

"This is it," Kael said, his voice filled with awe. "The Heart of the Temple. The gem is said to hold the essence of the gods, a fragment of their power."

Elara's eyes widened with understanding. "To pass the trial, we must prove our worthiness to the gods," she said, her voice steady. "We must show them that we are worthy of the Crown of Midnight Stars."

With a shared nod, they approached the pedestal, their hearts alight with determination. The gem pulsed with a divine light, its brilliance casting a warm glow upon their faces. Suddenly, the chamber trembled, and the mural on the ceiling came to life, the gods and demons locked in a celestial battle that seemed to spill into the very room.

"The gods are testing us," Seraphine said, her eyes wide with realization. "We must prove our courage and conviction in the face of their trials."

The gods' trial came in the form of a series of illusions, each one testing a different aspect of their character. Elara faced an illusion of her past, reliving the pain of her losses and the weight of her responsibilities. Seraphine confronted an illusion of her fears, facing the possibility of failure and the doubts that haunted her deepest thoughts. Kael, too, faced his own illusions, reliving the moments of his past that filled him with regret and longing.

But they refused to succumb to the illusions. With every trial, they stood firm, their minds and hearts unyielding against the gods' tests. The chamber seemed to vibrate with their determination, as if acknowledging their unwavering resolve.

At last, the illusions faded, leaving them standing before the gem, their breaths ragged and their bodies weary from the ordeal. The gem pulsed with a blinding light, its brilliance filling the chamber with a divine glow. With a sense of reverence, Elara reached out, her fingers brushing against the gem's surface.

Suddenly, the temple trembled once more, and the chamber seemed to dissolve into a blinding light. When the brilliance faded, they found themselves standing in a different place—a vast, celestial realm bathed in the glow of countless stars.

Before them stood the gods, their forms majestic and awe-inspiring. Their eyes, like infinite galaxies, gazed upon them with a mixture of curiosity and approval.

"You have proven your worthiness," one of the gods said, their voice a melodic blend of wind and water. "You have faced our trials and emerged victorious. The Crown of Midnight Stars is yours to claim."

With a sense of awe, Elara, Seraphine, and Kael accepted the gem, its divine power filling them with a sense of purpose and determination. The gods' realm seemed to fade away, and they found themselves back in the grand chamber, the gem glowing brightly in their hands.

"We have it," Seraphine said, her voice filled with wonder. "The Heart of the Temple."

Elara nodded, her heart pounding with a mix of excitement and trepidation. The suspense of their journey had reached its peak, and the final trial was now behind them. The Crown

of Midnight Stars was within their grasp, its power a beacon of hope in the face of darkness.

With the gem in their possession, they made their way back to the temple's entrance, their steps light with the knowledge of their success. As they emerged into the night, the stars seemed to shine brighter, as if celebrating their victory.

But unknown to them, shadows moved in the periphery of their vision, and unseen forces watched their progress with keen interest. The world was on the brink of change, and the Crown of Midnight Stars held the key to its fate. Little did they know that their actions would echo through the ages, shaping the course of history in ways they could scarcely imagine.

And so, with the weight of the world on their shoulders, they set forth once more, their hearts alight with the fire of purpose and the knowledge that their journey was far from over. The suspense of their quest had reached its climax, and the fate of the world hung in the balance. But they were undeterred, their resolve unbreakable as they prepared to face the challenges that lay ahead.

The final chapter of their tale was yet to be written, and the true test of their courage and conviction was yet to come. And so, beneath the starlit sky, they pressed on, their destinies intertwined in a tapestry of magic and destiny. The world awaited their actions, and the suspense of their journey continued, the story of the Crown of Midnight Stars unfolding with each step they took into the unknown.

The Final Confrontation

The night was shrouded in a cloak of tension as Elara, Seraphine, and Kael made their way toward the fabled location revealed to them by the Heart of the Temple. The gem they now possessed pulsed with an ethereal light, illuminating their path through the dense forest. Their footsteps were muffled by the thick layer of fallen leaves, and the air was thick with the scent of ancient magic.

Their destination was the Eclipse Altar, a sacred site at the nexus of mystical ley lines. It was said to be the place where the Crown of Midnight Stars could be awakened and its true power harnessed. As they approached the altar, the very ground seemed to tremble beneath their feet, as if in anticipation of the momentous events about to unfold.

The Eclipse Altar loomed before them, a monolithic structure adorned with intricate runes and symbols that glowed with an otherworldly light. At its center lay a dais, upon which rested a pedestal designed to cradle the Heart of the Temple—a receptacle for the gem's divine power.

Elara, Seraphine, and Kael approached the altar with a mixture of trepidation and determination. The suspense of their journey had led them to this pivotal moment, the culmination of their trials and tribulations. The fate of the world hung in the balance, and the burden of their responsibility weighed heavily on their shoulders.

With a sense of reverence, Elara placed the gem onto the pedestal. Instantly, a surge of energy enveloped the altar, illuminating the forest with a radiant glow. The very stars above seemed to respond, their brilliance intensifying as if acknowledging the awakening of a great power.

But their moment of awe was interrupted by a sinister presence that slithered through the air like a shadowy serpent. A figure emerged from the darkness—a sorcerer of immense power, his eyes ablaze with a malevolent light.

"Elara, Seraphine, Kael," the sorcerer said, his voice a cold whisper that sent chills down their spines. "You've played your part well, but the Crown of Midnight Stars belongs to me."

It was Alistair, the rival mage they had thought defeated in the depths of the River of Shadows. His presence was an unsettling reminder of the dangers that lurked in the shadows, and his hunger for power was evident in the twisted grin that curved his lips.

"You're too late, Alistair," Elara said, her voice steady despite the rising tension. "The Crown of Midnight Stars will not fall into the hands of someone like you."

Alistair's laughter echoed through the clearing, a sound devoid of warmth or humanity. "You underestimate me," he said, his eyes narrowing with determination. "I will harness the power of the crown and reshape the world according to my will. No one can stop me."

With a wave of his hand, Alistair unleashed a torrent of dark energy, its tendrils snaking toward the gem on the pedestal. Elara, Seraphine, and Kael sprang into action, their own magic forming a barrier to protect the Heart of the Temple. The clash of their spells filled the air with crackling energy, the suspense escalating with every moment.

The battle that ensued was a symphony of magic and willpower, a contest of strength and determination that shook the very foundations of the Eclipse Altar. Alistair's spells were potent and unpredictable, his mastery over the dark arts evident in the way he twisted reality to his advantage. Elara, Seraphine, and Kael fought back with unwavering resolve, their determination to protect the gem unyielding.

The suspense reached a fever pitch as the battle raged on, the fate of the world hanging in the balance. Spells collided, sending shockwaves through the clearing. The very ground trembled beneath the force of their magic, and the air crackled with the intensity of their conflict.

In a moment of desperation, Alistair unleashed a forbidden spell—a dark incantation that threatened to consume everything in its path. Elara, Seraphine, and Kael combined their powers, their magic forming a brilliant counter-spell that clashed with Alistair's darkness.

The explosion that followed was blinding, a burst of light that engulfed the entire clearing. When the brilliance faded, the three mages found themselves standing in a smoldering crater, their breaths ragged and their bodies bruised from the onslaught.

But Alistair was nowhere to be seen. The force of their combined counter-spell had sent him fleeing into the depths of the forest, his defeat a testament to their strength and unity.

"We did it," Seraphine said, her voice filled with a mixture of relief and triumph. "Alistair is gone, and the gem is safe."

Elara nodded, her eyes fixed on the Heart of the Temple. The suspense of their confrontation with Alistair had reached its climax, and they had emerged victorious. But their journey was not over. The Crown of Midnight Stars awaited its final awakening, and the true test of their courage and conviction was yet to come.

With a shared determination, they turned their attention back to the gem. The time had come to awaken the crown's power and fulfill the ancient prophecy. Elara, Seraphine, and Kael channeled their magic, their energies intertwining with the divine essence of the gem.

A brilliant light enveloped the Eclipse Altar, illuminating the entire forest with its radiant glow. The stars above seemed to respond, their brilliance intensifying as if in harmony with the awakening power below. The suspense of the moment was palpable, a tangible force that sent shivers down their spines.

Suddenly, the gem shattered, its fragments merging with the very fabric of the universe. The ground trembled beneath their feet, and a surge of energy washed over them, filling them with a power beyond imagination. The suspense of the moment gave way to a sense of awe and wonder, their hearts alight with the brilliance of the crown's awakening.

"We've done it," Kael said, his voice filled with reverence. "The Crown of Midnight Stars is awakened."

Elara's eyes shone with determination. "Now, we must use its power wisely. It's not just a source of magic—it's a force that can shape the world. We must protect it and ensure it's never misused."

Seraphine nodded, her expression resolute. "We'll guard it with our lives if we must. The world deserves a future free from darkness."

And so, beneath the starlit sky, the three mages stood at the Eclipse Altar, their destinies intertwined with the Crown of Midnight Stars. The suspense of their journey had reached its resolution, and a new chapter in the history of the world was about to begin.

Little did they know that their actions

would echo through the ages, shaping the course of history in ways they could scarcely imagine. The suspense of their adventure had led them to this pivotal moment, and the world awaited their guidance with bated breath.

With the Crown of Midnight Stars in their hands, they set forth, their hearts alight with the fire of purpose and the knowledge that they had the power to change the world. The suspense of their journey had come to an end, but the story of the Crown of Midnight Stars was far from over.

And so, beneath the stars that had witnessed their trials and triumphs, they ventured into the unknown, their hearts ablaze with the hope of a brighter future. The suspense of their past adventures lingered in their memories, a reminder of the challenges they had overcome. But they were undeterred, their resolve unbreakable as they prepared to face whatever new challenges lay ahead.

The world was now in their hands, and the suspense of the future beckoned them forward, into a world where their actions would shape the destiny of generations to come. And so, with courage in their hearts and magic at their fingertips, they embraced the unknown, their journey continuing into the endless expanse of possibilities.

The Shadow's Return

The world had changed since the awakening of the Crown of Midnight Stars. The air was charged with a newfound energy, and the very fabric of reality seemed to ripple with the echoes of ancient power. Elara, Seraphine, and Kael, the guardians of the Crown, had become symbols of hope and strength in a world that had been plagued by darkness for far too long.

But the peace they had fought so hard to achieve was fragile, a delicate balance between light and shadow. The suspense of the unknown hung heavy in the air, for there were whispers of a looming threat—a force that sought to harness the power of the Crown for nefarious purposes.

In a hidden fortress shrouded in secrecy, a shadowy figure known only as the Shadow Weaver plotted and schemed. His eyes glowed with an unnatural hunger, and his fingers danced with dark magic. He had witnessed the awakening of the Crown of Midnight Stars, and his obsession with its power consumed him.

"I will have the Crown," he muttered to himself, his voice a whisper that seemed to carry on the wind. "Its power will be mine, and the world will bow before my might."

With a wave of his hand, he summoned his most loyal followers—mages and warriors corrupted by his dark influence. Their eyes glowed with an eerie light, and their hearts beat in sync with the Shadow Weaver's nefarious desires.

"Our time is at hand," the Shadow Weaver said, his voice echoing through the shadowy chamber. "We will strike when the guardians least expect it, and the Crown will be ours."

Meanwhile, Elara, Seraphine, and Kael were not oblivious to the growing threat. The suspense of their days was tinged with vigilance, their senses alert to the subtlest signs of danger. They knew that their victory over Alistair was but a prelude to a greater challenge—one that would test their strength and unity to the utmost.

One fateful night, as the moon hung low in the sky, the guardians received a cryptic message—a warning from an ancient seer who dwelled in the depths of an enchanted forest. The seer's words were laden with urgency, her voice a haunting melody that echoed in their minds.

"The Shadow Weaver seeks the Crown," the seer said, her eyes clouded with visions of the future. "He will stop at nothing to claim its power. Beware his cunning and his dark magic, for he will strike when the moon is at its darkest."

The guardians exchanged solemn glances, the weight of the seer's words settling upon their shoulders like a heavy burden. The suspense of their mission deepened, and a sense of foreboding gripped their hearts.

"We must confront the Shadow Weaver before he can unleash his plans," Elara said, her voice firm despite the uncertainty that gnawed at her. "We cannot allow the Crown to fall into his hands."

With a shared determination, they set forth on a perilous journey, their path guided by the seer's cryptic visions. The suspense of their quest was palpable, each step forward laden with the anticipation of an inevitable confrontation.

Their journey led them through enchanted forests and treacherous mountains, their senses attuned to the slightest disturbances in the natural order. The suspense of their surroundings was heightened by the eerie silence that seemed to hang in the air, broken only by the occasional rustle of leaves or the distant howl of a wolf.

At last, they arrived at the edge of a desolate wasteland—a barren expanse of twisted trees and ashen soil. The very ground seemed to crack beneath their feet, as if scorched by an ancient fire. In the heart of this wasteland stood the Shadow Weaver's fortress—a towering structure of obsidian and shadow.

The guardians approached the fortress with caution, their eyes scanning its dark spires for any signs of movement. The suspense of their impending confrontation weighed heavily on their minds, and the air seemed to vibrate with an undercurrent of dark magic.

As they entered the fortress, the air grew thick with the scent of incense and decay. Shadows danced along the walls, their movements mirroring the guardians' every step. The suspense of their surroundings was suffocating, a tangible force that pressed upon their hearts.

At the heart of the fortress, they found the Shadow Weaver—a figure cloaked in darkness, his features obscured by a hooded robe. His eyes glowed with an unnatural light, and his fingers crackled with dark energy.

"So, you've come," the Shadow Weaver said, his voice a low hiss that seemed to slither through the air. "But you are too late. The Crown of Midnight Stars will be mine, and you shall bow before its power."

The suspense of the moment hung heavy in the air, a charged silence that seemed to stretch into eternity. Then, with a sudden burst of movement, the Shadow Weaver unleashed his magic—a torrent of darkness that swept toward the guardians like a tidal wave.

Elara, Seraphine, and Kael sprang into action, their own magic forming a protective barrier against the onslaught. The clash of their spells filled the chamber with blinding light and deafening noise, the suspense of their battle reaching a crescendo.

The battle that followed was like a tempest of magic and willpower, a clash of light and shadow that reverberated through the fortress. Elara's spells crackled with lightning, her magic striking with speed and precision. Seraphine summoned torrents of water and gusts of wind, her control over the elements a force to be reckoned with. Kael's knowledge of ancient spells proved invaluable, his incantations countering the Shadow Weaver's dark magic.

But the Shadow Weaver was no ordinary foe. His spells were cunning and unpredictable, his mastery over the shadows allowing him to slip through their defenses. The suspense of their battle escalated with every moment, each spell and counter-spell escalating the stakes.

In a desperate gambit, the Shadow Weaver conjured a sphere of pure darkness—a singularity that threatened to consume everything in its path. Elara, Seraphine, and Kael pooled their magic, their combined strength forming a brilliant counter-spell that clashed with the singularity.

The explosion that followed was deafening, a burst of light and darkness that shattered the very foundations of the fortress. When the brilliance faded, the guardians found themselves standing amidst the wreckage, their breaths ragged and their bodies bruised from the onslaught.

But the Shadow Weaver was not defeated. With a snarl of rage, he unleashed a final, devastating spell—an incantation that threatened to tear the very fabric of reality. The guardians, their energy depleted from the battle, struggled to counter the spell.

In their moment of desperation, a surge of power filled them—an echo of the Crown's awakening. With newfound strength, they channeled their magic, their energies intertwining with the divine essence of the Crown. A blinding light enveloped them, and their counter-spell surged forward, colliding with the Shadow Weaver's incantation.

The force of their combined magic was overwhelming, a cataclysmic explosion that consumed the entire chamber. The suspense of the moment reached its peak, and then, with a deafening roar, the darkness was dispelled, leaving behind a sense of eerie silence.

When the smoke cleared, the guardians found themselves standing amidst the ruins of the fortress. The Shadow Weaver was nowhere to be seen, his

dark presence vanquished by their combined might. The suspense of their battle had reached its climax, and they had emerged victorious.

But their victory came at a cost. The fortress lay in ruins, its once-mighty spires reduced to rubble. The very air seemed to mourn the destruction, carrying with it the weight of the battles fought within its walls.

"We did it," Seraphine said, her voice filled with a mixture of relief and sorrow. "But at what cost?"

Elara's gaze was steely, her resolve unyielding. "We cannot afford to falter," she said, her voice firm. "The world depends on our strength and unity. We must protect the Crown of Midnight Stars at all costs."

And so, with the suspense of their battle still hanging in the air, the guardians pressed on, their determination unshaken by the challenges they had faced. The world was on the brink of change, and the Crown of Midnight Stars held the key to its fate. Little did they know that their actions would echo through the ages, shaping the course of history in ways they could scarcely imagine.

And so, with the weight of the world on their shoulders, they set forth once more, their hearts alight with the fire of purpose and the knowledge that their journey was far from over. The suspense of their adventure had reached its climax, and the fate of the world hung in the balance. But they were undeterred, their resolve unbreakable as they prepared to face the challenges that lay ahead.

The final chapter of their tale was yet to be written, and the true test of their courage and conviction was yet to come. And so, beneath the starlit sky, they pressed on, their destinies intertwined in a tapestry of magic and destiny. The world awaited their actions, and the suspense of their journey continued, the story of the Crown of Midnight Stars unfolding with each step they took into the unknown.

The Veil Between Worlds

The aftermath of the battle with the Shadow Weaver left the guardians weary but resolute. Their victory had come at a great cost, and the suspense of their journey had taken a toll on their spirits. Yet, they knew that their mission was far from over. The Crown of Midnight Stars, now safeguarded in a hidden chamber deep within the enchanted forest, was a beacon of hope in a world still shadowed by threats.

As they gathered under the sheltering branches of the ancient Elderwood Tree, their meeting place and sanctuary, a new sense of purpose filled the air. The suspense of the unknown loomed over them like a gathering storm, and they felt the weight of their responsibilities pressing upon their shoulders.

Elara, her eyes reflecting the wisdom of ages, spoke first. "We have safeguarded the Crown, but the world is still vulnerable. We must remain vigilant. There are forces beyond our understanding that seek to exploit the Crown's power."

Seraphine, her hair cascading like a waterfall of obsidian, nodded in agreement. "The barriers between our world and the realms beyond are thinning. Strange occurrences have been reported—unexplained phenomena that hint at a rift in the fabric of reality."

Kael, his eyes alight with the fervor of a scholar, interjected, "It could be related to the Crown. Its awakening may have unintended consequences, unraveling the natural order of things."

The suspense of their conversation hung in the air, each word spoken laden with the gravity of their situation. They knew that they had to delve deeper into the mysteries surrounding the Crown of Midnight Stars, for the fate of their world depended on their understanding of its true nature.

With a shared determination, they set out on a new quest—a journey to uncover the secrets of the Crown and the enigmatic forces that sought to exploit its power. Their path led them to the ancient libraries of the Arcane Order, repositories of knowledge that held the lore of ages long past.

The libraries were vast, their shelves lined with scrolls and tomes that seemed to stretch into infinity. The air was thick with the scent of old parchment and the faint tang of magic. The suspense of their search for answers was palpable, each whispering page holding the promise of enlightenment.

Days turned into weeks as they delved into the ancient texts, deciphering cryptic passages and studying forgotten rituals. The suspense of their discoveries was both exhilarating and unnerving, for the knowledge they unearthed revealed the existence of an ancient artifact—the Veilshroud Amulet.

According to the texts, the Veilshroud Amulet was a relic of immense power, crafted by the ancient sorcerers of the Eldergrove. It had the ability to mend the tears in the fabric of reality, bridging the gaps between worlds. The suspense of their realization settled upon them like a heavy cloak, for they knew that the amulet could be the key to understanding and potentially repairing the rifts they had sensed.

Their quest for the Veilshroud Amulet led them to the Whispering Marshes, a mist-laden realm where time seemed to stand still. The suspense of their surroundings was heightened by the eerie silence that enveloped the marshes, broken only by the distant calls of unseen creatures.

Navigating the marshes proved to be a daunting challenge, the ground treacherous with hidden bogs and quicksand. The suspense of their journey was intensified by the ever-watchful eyes of spectral will-o'-the-wisps, their ethereal glow illuminating the path ahead.

After days of painstaking search, they stumbled upon an ancient temple hidden amidst the marshes—a structure of moss-covered stone and crumbling arches. The suspense of their discovery was tempered by a sense of reverence, for they knew that the temple held the key to finding the Veilshroud Amulet.

Within the temple's depths, they found a chamber adorned with intricate murals depicting the sorcerers of the Eldergrove crafting the amulet. The suspense of their findings deepened as they deciphered the murals, revealing the steps needed to awaken the amulet's dormant power.

With bated breath, they followed the instructions, their magic intertwining with the ancient enchantments woven into the temple's walls. The suspense of their ritual was almost tangible, the air crackling with arcane energy.

As the last incantation left their lips, the chamber trembled, and a radiant glow enveloped the room. Suspense gave way to awe as the Veilshroud Amulet materialized before them—a delicate pendant adorned with a shimmering gem that seemed to hold the very essence of the cosmos.

With the amulet in their possession, they felt a surge of hope. The suspense of their journey had led them to a pivotal moment, and the fate of their world rested upon their shoulders. Armed with the amulet's power, they set out to mend the rifts in the fabric of reality, their steps guided by the whispers of the Eldergrove itself.

Their journey took them to the places where the veil between worlds was thinnest—a secluded glade where the boundaries of reality seemed to blur, and an ancient stone circle where ley lines converged. The suspense of their task weighed heavily upon them, for they knew that mending the fabric of reality required great skill and precision.

With the Veilshroud Amulet, they performed the ritual, their magic mingling with the amulet's power. The suspense of their actions was nerve-wracking, their every movement and incantation executed with utmost care.

As they completed the ritual, a brilliant light enveloped them, and the suspense of their efforts reached its peak. The very air seemed to tremble, and then, with a profound sense of relief, they witnessed the rifts in reality mend before their eyes.

The worlds beyond seemed to sigh in gratitude, the whispering winds carrying echoes of ancient voices. The suspense of their success was met with a profound sense of accomplishment, for they had averted a cataclysmic event that could have torn their world asunder.

But their victory was short-lived, for as they basked in the aftermath of their accomplishment, a sudden sense of dread settled upon them. The air grew cold, and the suspense of their surroundings deepened, for they sensed a malevolent presence—a force far darker than anything they had faced before.

A shadowy figure emerged from the depths of the glade—a being clad in tattered robes and crowned with horns like obsidian daggers. His eyes glowed with a sinister light, and his voice echoed with the whispers of a thousand lost souls.

"You have mended the veil between worlds," the figure intoned, his voice a chilling melody that sent shivers down their spines. "But you have also paved the way for my return."

The suspense of their encounter was suffocating, each word uttered by the figure laden with a sense of impending doom. They realized that they had unwittingly unleashed a force far beyond their understanding—a being that had been imprisoned beyond the rifts in reality.

With a wave of his hand, the figure conjured a vortex of shadow—a portal to the realm from which he had been banished. The suspense of their situation deepened as they realized the magnitude of their adversary.

"We must stop him," Elara said, her voice resolute. "We cannot allow him to return to our world and wreak havoc."

With a shared determination, they confronted the shadowy figure, their magic forming

a barrier against his dark power. The suspense of their battle was unlike anything they had experienced before, for the being seemed to draw strength from the very essence of the rifts they had mended.

The battle raged on, the suspense of their conflict reaching a fever pitch. Spells collided, sending shockwaves through the glade. The very ground trembled beneath the force of their magic, and the air crackled with the intensity of their struggle.

In a desperate gambit, the shadowy figure summoned tendrils of darkness that snaked toward the Veilshroud Amulet. The suspense of their moment of crisis gripped their hearts, for they knew that if the amulet fell into the being's hands, all would be lost.

With unwavering resolve, they channeled their magic, their energies intertwining with the amulet's power. The suspense of their struggle was palpable, each heartbeat echoing in the silence of the glade.

The clash that followed was cataclysmic, a torrent of light and shadow that seemed to consume the very fabric of reality. The suspense of their battle reached its zenith, and then, with a blinding flash, the shadowy figure was vanquished, his malevolent presence banished once more beyond the rifts in reality.

As the dust settled and the echoes of their battle faded, the guardians stood amidst the glade, their breaths ragged and their bodies bruised from the onslaught. The suspense of their victory was tempered by the knowledge that they had faced a force beyond imagination and emerged triumphant.

"We did it," Seraphine said, her voice filled with a mixture of relief and awe. "But the threat of the rifts remains. We must remain vigilant."

Elara nodded, her eyes reflecting the wisdom of ages. "Agreed. The fabric of reality is fragile, and we must safeguard it at all costs. Our world depends on it."

With a shared determination, they returned to the Elderwood Tree, their steps heavy with the weight of their responsibilities. The suspense of their encounter lingered in the air, a reminder of the challenges they had faced and the ones that lay ahead.

And so, beneath the shadowed canopy of the Elderwood Tree, they gathered once more, their hearts alight with the fire of purpose and the knowledge that their journey was far from over. The suspense of their adventure had reached its climax, and the fate of the world hung in the balance. But they were undeterred, their resolve unbreakable as they prepared to face the challenges that lay ahead.

The final chapter of their tale was yet to be written, and the true test of their courage and conviction was yet to come. And so, beneath the starlit sky, they pressed on, their destinies intertwined in a tapestry of magic and destiny.

The world awaited their actions, and the suspense of their journey continued, the story of the Crown of Midnight Stars unfolding with each step they took into the unknown.

The Forgotten Prophecy

The land was draped in an eerie silence, broken only by the faint rustle of leaves and the distant hoot of an owl. The guardians, Elara, Seraphine, and Kael, stood at the edge of the Enchanted Abyss—a vast chasm that seemed to stretch into infinity. The suspense of their surroundings was palpable, a shroud of mystery and foreboding that clung to the very air.

Before them, suspended on an ornate pedestal, lay the Scroll of Eternity—an ancient artifact that held the forgotten prophecies of the Eldergrove. Its parchment was as delicate as spider silk, its inked symbols glowing with a soft, ethereal light. The suspense of their mission weighed heavily upon them, for they knew that the Scroll held the key to unraveling the mysteries that still eluded them.

Elara, her eyes glinting with determination, reached out to touch the Scroll. The moment her fingers brushed the parchment, the room seemed to come alive with a surge of energy. The suspense of their discovery was electrifying, each symbol on the Scroll pulsating with a life of its own.

As she began to read the prophecies aloud, the guardians listened with bated breath, their hearts quickening with anticipation. The suspense of the words washed over them, painting vivid images of a future yet to unfold—a future that seemed both ominous and full of hope.

"In the twilight of worlds, when shadows dance with the stars, a great evil shall awaken," Elara intoned, her voice echoing in the chamber. "Three champions, marked by destiny, shall rise to challenge the darkness. Their hearts, entwined with courage and sacrifice, shall determine the fate of all realms."

The suspense of the prophecy settled upon them like a heavy fog, its words laden with the weight of inevitability. They knew that they were the champions spoken of in the Scroll, chosen by fate to face an unimaginable threat.

"The Crown of Midnight Stars, a beacon of light in the void, shall guide their way," Elara continued, her eyes flickering with the reflection of the Scroll's glow. "But to harness its true power, they must confront the trials of the Elemental Realms. Only then can the Crown's full potential be unlocked, and the world saved from eternal darkness."

The suspense of their mission deepened, for the Elemental Realms were ancient and enigmatic—a realm of primal forces and elemental magic, where challenges of the mind, body, and spirit awaited those who dared to tread its paths.

With a shared resolve, the guardians set forth on their journey to the Elemental Realms, their steps guided by the Scroll's cryptic instructions. The suspense of their passage through the veiled portals was both exhilarating and nerve-wracking, their surroundings shifting and morphing with each step.

First, they entered the Realm of Earth—a place of towering cliffs and labyrinthine caves, where the very ground trembled with the power of stone and rock. The suspense of their trials was immediate, as they faced challenges that tested their strength and perseverance. Massive boulders rolled toward them, and treacherous chasms yawned beneath their feet. Only by working together and using their wits did they emerge victorious, the suspense of their victory met with a sense of relief.

Next came the Realm of Air—a realm of endless skies and swirling storms, where the very air crackled with the energy of the tempest. The suspense of their trials in this realm was centered around agility and quick thinking. Fierce winds threatened to sweep them away, and lightning crackled across the sky, seeking to strike them down. Through sheer determination and strategic maneuvering, they overcame the challenges, the suspense of their success leaving them breathless.

The third realm they ventured into was the Realm of Fire—a realm of searing heat and molten rivers, where the very air shimmered with the intensity of the flames. The suspense of their trials here was a test of endurance and resilience. Walls of fire blocked their path, and lakes of lava threatened to consume them. With unwavering determination and a deep understanding of their own limits, they navigated the fiery trials, the suspense of their survival mingling with a sense of accomplishment.

Lastly, they entered the Realm of Water—a realm of unfathomable depths and raging torrents, where the very waves seemed to pulse with life. The suspense of their trials in this realm was a challenge of adaptability and ingenuity. Tsunamis threatened to engulf them, and deadly whirlpools threatened to drag them into the abyss. By harnessing the power of water and using their creativity, they outmaneuvered the challenges, the suspense of their victory met with a sense of awe.

Having triumphed over the trials of the Elemental Realms, the guardians returned to the material world, their bodies and minds bearing the marks of their ordeals. The suspense of their journey had transformed them, imbuing them with newfound strength and unity.

With the elemental challenges behind them, they turned their attention back to the Scroll of Eternity. The suspense of the prophecy weighed heavily upon them, its words a reminder of the great responsibility they bore.

"The final trial awaits," Seraphine said, her voice steady despite the suspense that hung in the air. "We must confront the great evil spoken of in the prophecy and ensure that darkness does not triumph."

With a shared determination, they set out on their final quest, guided by the Scroll's cryptic instructions. The suspense of their mission was heightened by the knowledge that the fate of the world rested upon their shoulders.

Their path led them to the Obsidian Citadel—a towering fortress that seemed to merge seamlessly with the darkened sky. The suspense of their approach was met with a sense of foreboding, for they knew that within the Citadel lay the heart of the darkness they sought to vanquish.

As they entered the Citadel, the suspense of their surroundings deepened. The air was thick with the scent of ancient magic, and the very walls seemed to pulse with a malevolent energy. Shadows danced along the corridors, their movements mirroring the guardians' every step.

At the heart of the Citadel, they found the source of the darkness—a figure clad in obsidian armor, his eyes ablaze with an unholy light. He was Azaroth, the harbinger of the great evil foretold in the prophecy. The suspense of their encounter was suffocating, each word spoken by Azaroth laced with venom and malice.

"You have come far, little champions," Azaroth sneered, his voice echoing through the chamber. "But your journey ends here. The darkness shall consume you, and the world shall bow before its might."

The suspense of their confrontation reached its peak, and with a shared determination, the guardians faced Azaroth. Their magic clashed with his dark power, filling the chamber with blinding light and deafening noise. The suspense of their battle was like a tempest, a clash of light and shadow that reverberated through the Citadel.

Spells collided, sending shockwaves through the chamber. The very walls trembled beneath the force of their magic, and the air crackled with the intensity of their conflict. The suspense of their struggle was palpable, each moment laden with the weight of

their choices and the outcome of their battle.

In a desperate gambit, Azaroth summoned a vortex of darkness—a singularity that threatened to consume everything in its path. The guardians, their energy depleted from the battle, struggled to counter the spell. The suspense of their moment of crisis gripped their hearts, for they knew that if they faltered, all would be lost.

But just as all hope seemed lost, a surge of power filled them—an echo of the Crown's awakening. With newfound strength, they channeled their magic, their energies intertwining with the divine essence of the Crown. A blinding light enveloped them, and their counter-spell surged forward, colliding with Azaroth's singularity.

The explosion that followed was deafening, a burst of light and darkness that shattered the very foundations of the Citadel. When the brilliance faded, the guardians found themselves standing amidst the ruins, their breaths ragged and their bodies bruised from the onslaught.

But Azaroth was not defeated. With a roar of rage, he unleashed a final, devastating spell—an incantation that threatened to tear the very fabric of reality. The guardians, their energy depleted from the battle, struggled to counter the spell.

In their moment of desperation, a surge of power filled them—an echo of the Crown's awakening. With newfound strength, they channeled their magic, their energies intertwining with the divine essence of the Crown. A blinding light enveloped them, and their counter-spell surged forward, colliding with

Azaroth's incantation.

The force of their combined magic was overwhelming, a cataclysmic explosion that consumed the entire chamber. The suspense of the moment reached its peak, and then, with a deafening roar, the darkness was dispelled, leaving behind a sense of eerie silence.

When the smoke cleared, the guardians found themselves standing amidst the ruins of the Citadel. Azaroth was nowhere to be seen, his dark presence vanquished by their combined might. The suspense of their battle had reached its climax, and they had emerged victorious.

But their victory came at a cost. The Citadel lay in ruins, its once-mighty spires reduced to rubble. The very air seemed to mourn the destruction, carrying with it the weight of the battles fought within its walls.

"We did it," Seraphine said, her voice filled with a mixture of relief and sorrow. "But at what cost?"

Elara's gaze was steely, her resolve unyielding. "We cannot afford to falter," she said, her voice firm. "The world depends on our strength and unity. We must protect the Crown of Midnight Stars at all costs."

And so, with the suspense of their battle still hanging in the air, the guardians pressed on, their determination unshaken by the challenges they had faced. The world was on the brink of change, and the Crown of Midnight Stars held the key to its fate. Little did they know that their actions would echo through the ages, shaping the course of history in ways they could scarcely imagine.

And so, with the weight of the world on their shoulders, they set forth once more, their hearts alight with the fire of purpose and the knowledge that their journey was far from over. The suspense of their adventure had reached its climax, and the fate of the world hung in the balance. But they were undeterred, their resolve unbreakable as they prepared to face the challenges that lay ahead.

The final chapter of their tale was yet to be written, and the true test of their courage and conviction was yet to come. And so, beneath the starlit sky, they pressed on, their destinies intertwined in a tapestry of magic and destiny. The world awaited their actions, and the suspense of their journey continued, the story of the Crown of Midnight Stars unfolding with each step they took into the unknown.

The Echoes of Destiny

The world was on the cusp of a new era, and the guardians, Elara, Seraphine, and Kael, stood at the precipice of a monumental decision. The suspense of their mission had reached its peak, for they knew that the fate of the world hinged on the choices they were about to make.

Before them stood the Crown of Midnight Stars, its ethereal glow casting flickering shadows across their faces. The suspense of their surroundings was heightened by the weight of their responsibilities. The power of the Crown pulsed in the air, an echo of ancient energies that had shaped the very fabric of reality.

"We've come so far," Seraphine murmured, her voice a whisper amidst the suspense that hung in the chamber. "But the path ahead is shrouded in uncertainty. How do we use the Crown's power to ensure a future of peace and light?"

Elara, her eyes reflecting the wisdom of ages, nodded in understanding. "The Crown is both a beacon of hope and a source of immense power," she said, her voice steady. "We must wield it wisely, for its influence could either usher in an age of prosperity or plunge the world into darkness once more."

Kael, his gaze fixed on the Crown, added, "We must also be vigilant. There will always be those who seek to exploit its power for nefarious purposes.

The suspense of our decisions lies in striking a balance between safeguarding the Crown and using its magic to protect the world."

With a shared determination, they reached out, their fingertips brushing against the Crown's surface. The moment their skin made contact with the ancient artifact, a surge of energy coursed through them, filling the chamber with a soft, otherworldly light. The suspense of their connection with the Crown was both exhilarating and daunting, for they could feel its power resonating with the depths of their souls.

In that moment, a vision washed over them—a tapestry of images and emotions that spanned the ages. The suspense of the vision was overwhelming, each scene flashing before their eyes like fragments of a half-remembered dream.

They saw the founding of cities and the forging of alliances, the suspense of ancient battles and the triumph of heroes. They witnessed the rise and fall of empires, the suspense of lost civilizations and the birth of new ones. And woven amidst these moments were the echoes of their own journey—the trials they had faced, the sacrifices they had made, and the victories they had achieved.

But amidst the visions of hope, there were also glimpses of darkness—the suspense of looming threats and the shadows of past evils. They saw the faces of those who had fallen, the places scarred by conflict, and the hearts burdened by sorrow. The suspense of these moments served as a reminder of the challenges that still lay ahead.

As the vision faded, they found themselves back in the chamber, their hearts heavy with the knowledge of the choices they had to make. The suspense of their decisions weighed upon them, for they knew that the destiny of the world was in their hands.

"We must use the Crown's power to mend the wounds of the past and usher in a new era of peace," Elara said, her voice resolute. "But we must also remain vigilant. The suspense of our actions lies in staying true to our purpose and protecting the world from those who would seek to exploit the Crown's magic."

Seraphine nodded, her determination mirrored in her eyes. "We have faced unimaginable challenges together, and our bond is our greatest strength. The suspense of our unity is what will guide us in the face of adversity."

Kael, his voice steady, added, "Let us not forget the lessons of the past—the echoes of history that remind us of the consequences of unchecked power. The suspense of our wisdom lies in learning from the mistakes of those who came before us."

With their resolve fortified, they focused their minds and channeled their magic into the Crown of Midnight Stars. The suspense of their actions was electrifying, the air crackling with energy as they wove their intentions into the ancient artifact.

The Crown responded, its glow intensifying as it absorbed their magic. The suspense of their connection with the artifact deepened, and for a moment, time seemed to stand still.

Then, with a blinding flash, the Crown unleashed its power—a wave of pure, celestial light that spread across the world. The suspense of their moment of transformation gripped their hearts, for they could feel the energy of the Crown merging with the very essence of their beings.

In that moment, they became something more than themselves—beacons of hope and guardians of light. The suspense of their transformation was both awe-inspiring and humbling, for they knew that they had been chosen to safeguard the world from the forces of darkness.

With their newfound power, they set forth to mend the wounds of the world. The suspense of their mission was met with a deep sense of purpose, for they knew that their actions would shape the course of history.

They traveled to war-torn lands, bringing healing and restoration wherever they went. The suspense of their presence was met with gratitude and hope, as cities rebuilt and communities flourished under their guidance.

They confronted ancient evils and vanquished malevolent spirits that had plagued the world for centuries. The suspense of their battles was met with fierce determination, for they knew that they were the world's last line of defense against the darkness.

They brokered

peace treaties and forged alliances between warring factions, the suspense of their diplomacy met with sighs of relief and tears of joy. The world slowly began to heal, and the echoes of their actions reverberated across the continents.

But amidst the suspense of their successes, there were still challenges to face. The shadows of the past lingered, and new threats emerged to test their resolve. The suspense of their struggles was met with unwavering determination, for they knew that their journey was far from over.

And so, under the vast expanse of the starlit sky, they pressed on, their steps guided by the echoes of destiny. The suspense of their adventure continued, for the world was vast and ever-changing, and they were its guardians— bound by duty, driven by courage, and united by the enduring hope that their actions would pave the way for a future of peace and light.

As they stood together, gazing out at the horizon, the suspense of the unknown filled their hearts. But they faced it with unwavering determination, for they knew that as long as they stood united, the world would always have a glimmer of hope to light its darkest hours.

And so, the guardians ventured forth, their footsteps echoing in the sands of time. The suspense of their legacy lingered in the air, for they had become legends—heroes whose names would be whispered in awe and gratitude for generations to come. Their tale was etched into the annals of history, a testament to the power of unity, courage, and the enduring belief that even in the face of the greatest darkness, the light of hope would always prevail.

Whispers of the Abyss

In the tranquil days that followed their victory, the world basked in the glow of the guardians' accomplishments. Cities flourished, trade routes reopened, and laughter echoed in the streets. Yet, amidst the apparent peace, an unsettling tension lingered—a whisper of unease that drifted through the air like a shadowy specter.

The guardians, Elara, Seraphine, and Kael, felt the suspense of this disquiet keenly. Their days were spent in watchful vigilance, their minds attuned to the slightest disturbance in the delicate balance they had fought so hard to restore. The Crown of Midnight Stars, now a symbol of hope and stability, lay protected in the heart of the Elderwood Tree. Its ethereal light bathed the sanctuary in a soft, comforting glow, but the suspense of its presence was a constant reminder of the responsibility that came with wielding its power.

One evening, as the sun dipped below the horizon and the first stars began to twinkle in the night sky, a sense of foreboding settled over the guardians. The suspense of their intuition told them that something was amiss, a feeling that crawled under their skin like a swarm of restless insects.

"It's too quiet," Seraphine murmured, her voice barely audible above the rustle of leaves in the evening breeze. "The suspense of this silence—it feels unnatural."

Elara nodded in agreement, her eyes scanning the horizon with a watchful gaze. "I sense a disturbance in the magical currents," she said, her voice carrying the weight of her experience. "The suspense of this disturbance—it speaks of a darkness we haven't encountered before."

Kael, his brow furrowed in deep concentration, added, "We should investigate. The suspense of our inaction could lead to consequences we cannot afford."

With a shared resolve, they set out into the night, their footsteps silent against the forest floor. The suspense of their journey was palpable, their senses heightened as they navigated the shadows that clung to the edges of their vision. The world seemed to hold its breath, waiting for the impending revelation that lurked just beyond the veil of darkness.

As they ventured deeper into the woods, the suspense of their surroundings intensified. Strange whispers echoed through the trees, their voices layered with malice and ancient knowledge. The guardians exchanged uneasy glances, their senses tingling with the suspense of an unseen presence.

A sudden chill filled the air, and the forest seemed to come alive with an ominous energy. The suspense of their encounter with the unknown sent shivers down their spines, and they tightened their grips on their weapons, ready for whatever threat awaited them.

Emerging from the shadows came a figure—a silhouette cloaked in darkness, its eyes glinting with an eerie light. The suspense of their encounter with this enigmatic stranger hung in the air, for they could sense the power that emanated from the being before them.

"You guardians of light," the figure intoned, its voice a chilling whisper that slithered through the night. "You have disrupted the balance of the realms. The suspense of your actions has awakened forces that should have remained dormant."

Elara stepped forward, her gaze unwavering. "Who are you, and what do you want?" she demanded, her voice steady despite the suspense that coiled in her chest.

The figure chuckled—a sound like the rustle of dead leaves on a cold winter's night. "I am known as the Veilweaver," it said, its tone dripping with disdain. "I am the keeper of secrets, the guardian of forgotten knowledge. The suspense of your meddling has awakened an ancient entity—an abyssal force that hungers for power."

The guardians exchanged uneasy glances, the suspense of the Veilweaver's words sinking in. "What do you mean?" Seraphine asked, her voice tinged with apprehension. "What is this abyssal force, and how do we stop it?"

The Veilweaver's eyes glowed brighter, its form flickering like a dying candle in the wind. "The suspense of your questions is irrelevant," it hissed. "What you need to know is this: the abyssal force seeks to consume the world, plunging it into eternal darkness. It is drawn to the Crown of Midnight Stars, its hunger insatiable."

The guardians felt a knot of dread tighten in their chests. The suspense of the situation weighed heavily upon them, for they knew that the Crown, once a beacon of hope, could now attract a force of unimaginable darkness.

"We cannot allow this abyssal force to gain access to the Crown," Kael said, his voice firm. "The suspense of our duty as guardians is to protect it at all costs."

The Veilweaver's lips curled into a malevolent smile. "Then prepare yourselves," it said, its voice echoing with the suspense of impending doom. "The abyssal force approaches, drawn by the Crown's magic. It will stop at nothing to claim its power."

With those words, the Veilweaver vanished into the shadows, leaving the guardians with a sense of urgency that spurred them into action. The suspense of their mission was clear—they had to defend the Crown of Midnight Stars from this abyssal threat, no matter the cost.

They returned to the Elderwood Tree, the suspense of their footsteps echoing in the hushed stillness of the night. The Crown glowed softly, its light a beacon amidst the encroaching darkness. The guardians gathered around it, their minds intertwined in a web of determination and magic.

"We must strengthen the protective wards around the Crown," Elara said, her voice carrying the weight of their shared responsibility. "The suspense of our actions will be the last line of defense against the abyssal force."

With a shared focus, they channeled their magic into the protective wards, reinforcing the ancient spells that safeguarded the Crown. The suspense of their concentration was palpable, their energies intertwining with the very essence of the artifact.

Outside, the forest came alive with a cacophony of sinister whispers, the suspense of the abyssal force growing stronger with each passing moment. The guardians gritted their teeth, their determination unyielding in the face of the impending threat.

And then, with a deafening roar, the abyssal force descended upon them—a tidal wave of darkness that crashed against the protective wards with a force that threatened to shatter the very fabric of reality. The suspense of their battle with the abyssal force was overwhelming, each clash of magic sending shockwaves through the sanctum.

The guardians fought with unmatched determination, their spells colliding with the abyssal force's power in a dazzling display of light and shadow. The suspense of their struggle was like a tempest, a clash of elemental forces that reverberated through the sanctum.

But the abyssal force was relentless, its hunger insatiable. The suspense of their defenses wavered under the onslaught, and the guardians felt their strength beginning to falter. Sweat trickled down their brows, their breaths coming in ragged gasps as they poured every ounce of their energy into holding the line.

Just when it seemed like all hope was lost, a surge of power filled them— an echo of the Crown's magic. With newfound strength, they pushed back against the abyssal force, their spells gaining momentum as they drove the darkness back.

The suspense of their counterattack was met with a howl of rage from the abyssal force, its form contorting and writhing like a wounded beast. The guardians pressed their advantage, their determination unyielding as they fought with renewed vigor.

In a final, desperate gambit, the abyssal force unleashed a torrent of shadowy tendrils that snaked toward the Crown. The suspense of their moment of crisis gripped their hearts, for they knew that if the Crown fell into the abyssal force's hands, all would be lost.

With unwavering resolve, they channeled their magic, their energies intertwining with the Crown's power. The suspense of their struggle was palpable, each heartbeat echoing in the silence of the sanctum.

The clash that followed was cataclysmic, a torrent of light and shadow that seemed to consume the very sanctum itself. The suspense of their battle reached its zenith, and then, with a blinding flash, the abyssal force was vanquished, its malevolent presence banished once more into the depths of the abyss.

As the echoes of their battle faded, the guardians stood amidst the sanctum, their breaths ragged and their bodies bruised from the onslaught. The suspense of their victory was tempered by the knowledge that they had faced a force beyond imagination and emerged triumphant.

"We did it," Seraphine said, her voice filled with a mixture of relief and awe. "But the threat of the abyssal force remains. We must remain vigilant."

Elara nodded, her eyes reflecting the wisdom of ages. "Agreed. The abyssal force was merely a symptom of a larger problem. The suspense of our duty as guardians is far from over."

With a shared determination, they returned to their respective posts, the suspense of their encounter with the abyssal force lingering in the air. The world was safe for now, but they knew that the shadows of the abyss would always linger at the edges of their reality, waiting for a chance to strike.

And so, under the canopy of the Elderwood Tree, they stood once more, their hearts alight with the fire of purpose and the knowledge that their journey was far from over. The suspense of their adventure had reached its climax, and the fate of the world hung in the balance. But they were undeterred, their resolve unbreakable as they prepared to face the challenges that lay ahead.

The final chapter of their tale was yet to be written, and the true test of their courage and conviction was yet to come. And so, beneath the starlit sky, they pressed on, their destinies intertwined in a tapestry of magic and destiny. The world awaited their actions, and the suspense of their journey continued, the story of the Crown of Midnight Stars unfolding with each step they took into the unknown.

Little did they know that their actions had not gone unnoticed. Far beyond the reaches of their world, in the depths of the abyss from which the darkness had emerged, an ancient being stirred—a being whose power eclipsed even that of the abyssal force they had just vanquished.

The suspense of its awakening sent ripples through the fabric of reality, its malevolent gaze fixed upon the guardians and the Crown of Midnight Stars. In the dark corners of its mind, a plan began to form—a plan that would test the guardians' strength and resilience in ways they could not imagine.

And so, as the guardians continued their journey, blissfully unaware of the looming threat, the ancient being plotted in the shadows, its anticipation growing with each passing moment. The suspense of their encounter was inevitable, for the fate of the world hung in the balance, and the Crown of Midnight Stars held the key to both its salvation and its destruction.

The guardians had faced many challenges, but little did they know that their greatest test was yet to come—a test that would push them to their limits and force them to confront the very essence of darkness itself. The suspense of their destiny was entwined with the fate of the world, and the echoes of their actions would resonate across the ages, shaping the course of history in ways they could scarcely comprehend.

Veil of Shadows

The world had settled into a deceptive calm after the guardians' battle with the abyssal force. The Crown of Midnight Stars, once a beacon of hope, was now a focal point of suspense and apprehension. Its ethereal glow cast eerie shadows in the sanctum, and the guardians, Elara, Seraphine, and Kael, could sense the tension in the air—a palpable, suffocating suspense that clung to their every breath.

One fateful night, as the moon hung low in the sky, a shroud of darkness began to seep through the cracks of reality. The suspense of this encroaching shadow was unsettling, a harbinger of impending danger that crawled under their skin like a thousand tiny spiders. The sanctum, once a sanctuary, now seemed like a fragile fortress against an unknown foe.

Elara, her eyes alight with determination, paced the floor of the sanctum, her mind racing with thoughts of strategies and defenses. The suspense of the impending threat weighed heavily on her shoulders, for she knew that the world's fate rested upon their actions.

"We cannot afford to be caught off guard," she said, her voice steady despite the suspense that coiled in her chest. "We must strengthen the protective wards around the Crown and be prepared for whatever comes our way."

Seraphine nodded in agreement, her eyes reflecting the resolve that burned within her. "The suspense of our readiness will be our greatest asset," she said, her tone resolute. "We cannot allow the darkness to catch us unprepared."

Kael, his senses attuned to the mystical currents that flowed through the sanctum, added, "I sense a powerful presence beyond the veil of shadows—a being of immense darkness and malevolence. The suspense of this entity's power is unlike anything we've faced before."

With their roles defined and their determination steeled, they set to work fortifying the sanctum. The suspense of their preparations was intense, their minds focused on the task at hand. Protective wards were reinforced, ancient spells were woven into intricate patterns, and magical barriers were erected to repel any intrusion.

Outside, the suspense of the night deepened, the air thick with an other-worldly chill. Shadows danced along the trees, their movements mirroring the guardians' preparations within the sanctum. The world seemed to hold its breath, awaiting the clash between light and darkness that was sure to come.

As the final wards were put in place, a deafening crash reverberated through the sanctum, the suspense of the sound echoing in the guardians' ears. They turned as one, their eyes widening in shock as the veil of shadows parted to reveal the source of the disturbance—a towering figure clad in obsidian armor, its eyes ablaze with unholy light.

The suspense of their encounter with this menacing entity sent shivers down their spines. Its presence seemed to devour the very essence of the sanctum, leaving a void in its wake. It was a being of pure darkness—a Shadowlord, ancient and powerful, drawn by the allure of the Crown of Midnight Stars.

"You guardians have meddled in affairs that do not concern you," the

Shadowlord's voice echoed in the sanctum, the suspense of its words dripping with malice. "The Crown of Midnight Stars belongs to the shadows now. Surrender it, and your suffering will be swift."

Elara's eyes narrowed, her resolve unwavering. "We will never yield to the likes of you," she declared, her voice cutting through the suspense-laden air like a blade. "The Crown is a force of light, and we will protect it with our lives."

With a flick of its hand, the Shadowlord unleashed a wave of darkness that crashed against the sanctum's protective wards. The suspense of the impact sent shockwaves through the chamber, rattling the very foundations of their sanctuary. The guardians braced themselves, their combined magic pushing back against the relentless assault.

The suspense of their struggle was intense, the air crackling with the clash of opposing forces. The Shadowlord's laughter filled the sanctum, a sound that sent chills down their spines. "You may be strong, guardians, but the suspense of my power is boundless. Your futile resistance only prolongs your agony."

With those words, the Shadowlord intensified its assault, its dark energy seeping through the cracks in the protective wards. The suspense of their situation reached its peak, and the guardians knew that they had to find a way to repel this ancient menace.

Seraphine, her eyes blazing with determination, shouted, "We need to counter its darkness with our light! Channel your magic through the Crown, and let its power aid us in this battle!"

With a shared resolve, they focused their energies, their minds connecting with the Crown of Midnight Stars. The suspense of their connection with the ancient artifact sent tingles down their spines, and they felt its power surge through them like a torrential river.

In unison, they channeled their magic, their energies intertwining with the divine essence of the Crown. The suspense of their combined power filled the sanctum, illuminating the chamber with a brilliant, celestial light. The very air seemed to vibrate with the intensity of their magic.

The clash that followed was cataclysmic—a battle of light and shadow that shook the sanctum to its core. The suspense of their struggle was overwhelming, their magic colliding with the Shadowlord's power in a dazzling display of brilliance and darkness.

But the guardians were not alone in this battle. The Crown of Midnight Stars, now a conduit of their combined strength, bolstered their efforts with its ancient magic. The suspense of their connection with the artifact deepened, and they felt its power amplifying their own, turning them into beacons of hope amidst the encroaching darkness.

With renewed determination, they pushed back against the Shadowlord, their spells gaining momentum as they drove the darkness back. The suspense of their counterattack was met with a howl of rage from the Shadowlord, its form contorting and writhing like a wounded beast.

But the guardians pressed their advantage, their resolve unyield

ing as they fought with unwavering determination. The suspense of their unity was their greatest strength, and they knew that as long as they stood together, they could overcome any darkness.

In a final, desperate gambit, the Shadowlord unleashed a torrent of shadowy tendrils that snaked toward the Crown. The suspense of their moment of crisis gripped their hearts, for they knew that if the Crown fell into the Shadowlord's hands, all would be lost.

With unwavering resolve, they channeled their magic, their energies intertwining with the Crown's power. The suspense of their struggle was palpable, each heartbeat echoing in the silence of the sanctum.

The clash that followed was cataclysmic, a torrent of light and shadow that seemed to consume the very sanctum itself. The suspense of their battle reached its zenith, and then, with a blinding flash, the Shadowlord was vanquished, its malevolent presence banished once more into the depths of the abyss.

As the echoes of their battle faded, the guardians stood amidst the sanctum, their breaths ragged and their bodies bruised from the onslaught. The suspense of their victory was tempered by the knowledge that they had faced a force beyond imagination and emerged triumphant.

"We did it," Seraphine said, her voice filled with a mixture of relief and awe. "But the threat of the Shadowlord remains. We must remain vigilant."

Elara nodded, her eyes reflecting the wisdom of ages. "Agreed. The Shadowlord was merely a symptom of a larger problem. The suspense of our duty as guardians is far from over."

With a shared determination, they returned to their respective posts, the suspense of their encounter with the Shadowlord lingering in the air. The world was safe for now, but they knew that the shadows of the abyss would always linger at the edges of their reality, waiting for a chance to strike.

And so, under the canopy of the Elderwood Tree, they stood once more, their hearts alight with the fire of purpose and the knowledge that their journey was far from over. The suspense of their adventure had reached its climax, and the fate of the world hung in the balance. But they were undeterred, their resolve unbreakable as they prepared to face the challenges that lay ahead.

The final chapter of their tale was yet to be written, and the true test of their courage and conviction was yet to come. And so, beneath the starlit sky, they pressed on, their destinies intertwined in a tapestry of magic and destiny. The world awaited their actions, and the suspense of their journey continued, the story of the Crown of Midnight Stars unfolding with each step they took into the unknown.

But unknown to the guardians, in the aftermath of their battle, a subtle change had taken place within the Crown of Midnight Stars. Its ethereal glow, once a radiant beacon of hope, now held a shadowy undertone—a whisper of ancient power that hinted at a deeper, more profound truth.

As they stood beneath the Elderwood Tree, the suspense of their victory was tinged with a sense of foreboding. Elara, her eyes narrowed in contemplation, reached out to touch the Crown. The moment her fingertips made contact with its surface, a surge of energy coursed through her, sending shivers down her spine.

"The Crown has changed," she said, her voice filled with both awe and uncertainty. "Its power has evolved, as if it has absorbed the essence of the Shadowlord. The suspense of its transformation—it hints at something greater, something we may not fully comprehend."

Seraphine and Kael exchanged concerned glances, the suspense of Elara's revelation weighing heavily on their minds. The world was safe for now, but the Crown's transformation raised new questions, new uncertainties that added to the suspense of their already perilous journey.

"We must be cautious," Kael said, his voice a low murmur. "The Crown's new power may be a double-edged sword. The suspense of its potential—we cannot ignore the risks it may pose."

Seraphine nodded in agreement, her eyes fixed on the Crown. "We must learn to wield its new power responsibly," she said, her tone resolute. "The suspense of our choices will shape the future of the world."

With a shared understanding, they stepped back from the Crown, their minds filled with a mixture of curiosity and apprehension. The suspense of the Crown's transformation added a new layer of complexity to their mission, a challenge that tested their abilities and their resolve.

And so, as the night deepened and the stars glittered overhead, the guardians stood beneath the Elderwood Tree, their thoughts consumed by the suspense of the unknown. The world awaited their next steps, and the fate of the Crown of Midnight Stars remained intricately entwined with the destiny of the world itself.

Little did they know that their journey was far from over, and the suspense of their final challenge would push them to the very limits of their abilities. The true test of their courage and conviction was yet to come, and the fate of the world hung in the balance, suspended between the forces of light and darkness.

As they gazed up at the starlit sky, the suspense of their destiny weighed heavily upon them. But they were undeterred, their resolve unbreakable as they prepared to face the challenges that lay ahead. The final chapter of their tale was yet to be written, and the true meaning of the Crown of Midnight Stars was a mystery waiting to be unraveled—a suspenseful conclusion that would shape the fate of the world and the legacy of the guardians for generations to come.